Imitating *Nature*

From **Octopus Eyes** *to Powerful* **Lenses**

Toney Allman

KIDHAVEN PRESS

An imprint of Thomson Gale, a part of The Thomson Corporation

Detroit • New York • San Francisco • New Haven, Conn. • Waterville, Maine • London

LIBRARY OF CONGRESS CATALOGING-IN-PUBLICATION DATA

Allman, Toney.
From octopus eyes to powerful lenses / by Toney Allman.
     p. cm. — (Imitating nature)
Includes bibliographical references and index.
ISBN-13: 978-0-7377-3631-1 (hardcover : alk. paper)
ISBN-10: 0-7377-3631-3 (hardcover : alk. paper)
1.   Lenses—Juvenile literature. 2.   Optics—Juvenile literature.
3.   Octopuses—Juvenile literature.   I. Title.
QC385.A44 2007
535—dc22

2006018666

Printed in the United States of America

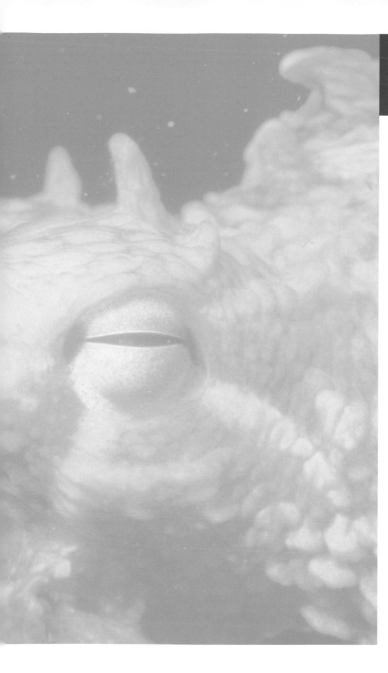

Contents

CHAPTER 1

Superior Octopus Eyes

Cameras and eyeglasses have something in common with the eyes of people and animals. All of them have to be able to **focus** sharply and clearly so that what they see is not blurry or fuzzy. Eric Baer leads a team of scientists at Case Western Reserve University in Ohio that is trying to make better cameras that imitate the eyes of an animal—the octopus. The team chose octopuses to copy because octopus eyes are extremely powerful.

Life as an Octopus

Octopuses live in oceans all around the world, except in the very coldest places. They can live in deep water, in shallow water, or around coral reefs. There are 289 different kinds of octopuses in the world. They range in size from as small as 2 inches (5 centimeters) to the 30-foot (9-meter) giant octopus of the Pacific.

Researchers are working on a camera that can focus as sharply as the powerful eyes of the octopus.

Octopuses come in various sizes and live in most of the world's ocean waters.

Smart Cookies

With mazes and puzzles, scientists have tested the intelligence of octopuses. They have determined that an octopus has the intelligence of a house cat.

The eyes of an octopus scan the ocean for food.

No matter what their size, all octopuses are **cephalopods**—soft-bodied animals with arms that surround their mouths. Other cephalopods include squid and cuttlefish. Octopuses are basically large, pouchlike heads surrounded by eight arms. They have no bones or skeletons. On the head are a hard, sharp beak for a mouth and two large eyes. Without the excellent sight of those eyes, an octopus could not survive. Octopuses use their eyesight to hunt for food, escape from enemies, and communicate with one another.

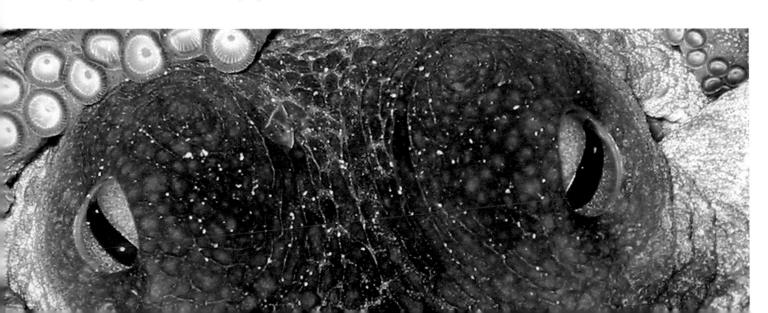

Eye Power in the Ocean

As most people have discovered, seeing under the water is more difficult than in the air. Water is thicker than air so it often makes objects look blurry. Sunlight shining into water creates glare. Rough, roiling waves can stir up mud and sand that cloud the water. None of these conditions bother octopuses, though. Their eyes see five times more sharply than human eyes. In bright sunshine, octopus eyes act like sunglasses, cutting out glare and making it possible to see comfortably.

Octopuses are predators that eat crabs, fish, and other sea creatures. A fish's scales can glare in the sunlight and disguise its position, but this is not a problem for an octopus. Its eyes accurately locate the fish, and the octopus can easily grab a meal with its

Most sea creatures such as this dolphin lack the sharp vision of the octopus.

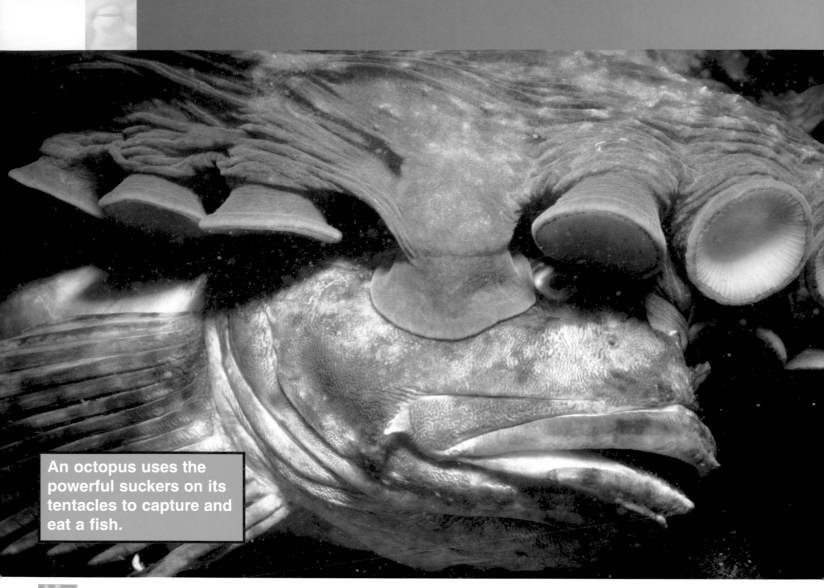

An octopus uses the powerful suckers on its tentacles to capture and eat a fish.

Feeling threatened, a frightened giant Pacific octopus shoots its inky cloud at a scuba diver.

arms. Crabs' shells may blend in with surrounding rocks and coral, but an octopus spies the animal with no difficulty and moves in quickly for the kill.

Octopuses are skillful predators, but other creatures consider octopuses to be tasty prey. Whales, sharks, large fish, and even birds prey on octopuses when they can. Octopuses use their good eyesight to spot predators so they can quickly escape. Often, a frightened octopus will release a cloud of inky fluid into the water when it is threatened by a predator.

Unusual Creatures

An octopus's brain is inside its stomach. It has three hearts and blue blood. Each of its arms can have up to 280 suckers on it that grab prey or cling to rocks with amazing strength. The arms also can remove lids from jars or a cork from a bottle to get at a fish inside. An octopus's arms and suckers have so many nerves in them that the octopus can actually taste with its suckers.

Octopus suckers

The ink confuses the predator and hides the octopus, but the octopus can see through its inky cloud and find the safe direction to flee. When it is crawling on its arms over the sea floor or swimming through the water, an octopus uses its eyes to avoid bumping into rocks or coral and harming itself. Since its soft body is not protected by a shell or bone, any injury could do great damage. The octopus keeps a sharp lookout for obstacles in its path.

The red coloring of this octopus suggests it is in a good mood.

From Octopus Eyes to Powerful Lenses

Octopus to Octopus

When two or more octopuses meet, they use an amazing method of signaling one another. Octopuses are able to change the colors of their bodies to communicate their moods. Although octopuses cannot see color, the change in shades is easily noticed by other octopuses. A red octopus, for example, is communicating pleasure or excitement, while a grayish-green one is calm and relaxed.

Octopus eyes clearly have astonishing abilities. Could people invent instruments that see as well as octopus eyes? Baer and his team thought they could if they just understood how octopus eyes work.

Octopus Tricks

Octopuses are not easy for people to control. An octopus is so smart, for example, that it can figure out how to lift the cover off its aquarium. At the New England Aquarium, a captive octopus crawled out of its tank every night to a nearby tank that was full of live fish. It gorged on the fish for weeks before it was discovered. A pet owner said that his octopus would climb out of the tank and come to him whenever he appeared with the octopus's meal. Octopuses have sneaked onto crabbing boats and then opened the holds and feasted on all the crabs.

CHAPTER 2

How Eyes Work

Vision works in about the same way for all kinds of eyes, whether they are animal eyes, human eyes, or artificial eyes. It is how the parts of the eyes are put together that determines how well someone or something can see. What happens when light enters an eye is what makes sight sharp or blurry.

To Catch a Wave

Light travels in waves. When a person sees, light waves bounce off an object and enter the **pupil** of the eye. The **iris expands** or **contracts** the pupil to let in more or less light, depending on how bright the light is. Then the light travels through the **lens** of the eye. The lens is clear and curved and made up of many layers. The curve of the lens bends the light to focus an image on the **retina**, which senses the light. The light is bent at a different angle for objects that are far away than for close ones. All images are blurry at first, because the light waves are not yet focused. But the

Human and animal eyes function in similar ways.

Light and the Human Eye

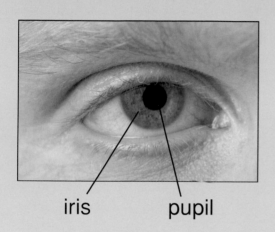

iris   pupil

1. Light waves enter the human eye through the curved lens.
2. The iris expands and contracts the pupil to let in more or less light.
3. The size of the pupil determines the amount of light that enters the eye.
4. The curve of the lens bends the light to focus an image on the retina.

Light enters the lens ▶▶▶▶▶▶▶▶▶▶

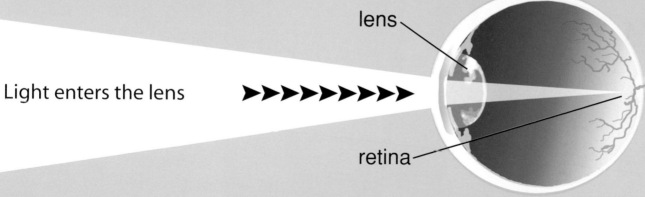

lens

retina

Humans rely on eyeglasses with carefully shaped lenses to correct vision defects.

lens fixes the blurriness and makes the image sharp. It does this with tiny muscles that change how much the lens is curved. The curve of the lens is what makes focusing possible. Some scientists call the lens the fine-tuner for the eye. When information from the eye travels to the brain, whatever the person is looking at appears clear and sharp.

When a person's lenses do not focus correctly, close-up or faraway images can look blurry. Then the person needs eyeglasses. These are curved glass or plastic lenses that focus light so the person can see sharply. Like water, however, glass and plastic can distort and bend light. The lenses must be carefully shaped to work properly.

Octopus Lenses

Octopus eyes work like human eyes, but there are differences. Human lenses, for example, are made up of about 22,000 layers. The layers bend light again and again until the image is sharp. Octopus lenses need more layers because light waves bend when they hit water and then scatter when they hit particles throughout the water. This makes it more difficult to focus and increases glare when sunshine reflects off objects in the water. To make up for these problems, octopus lenses have many thousands more layers than human eyes. They also have flat lenses that focus scattered light without being too big or heavy. The lenses move in and out to focus, somewhat like a camera's zoom lens, instead of changing shape with muscles like human lenses.

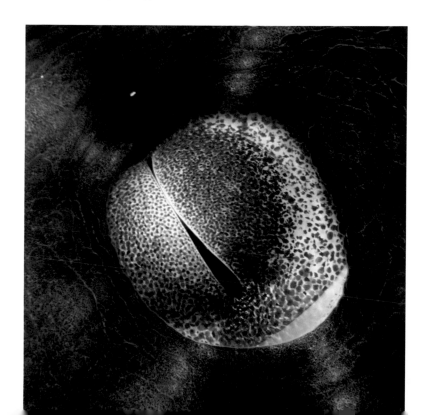

An octopus eye lens has many more layers than a human eye lens.

The Better to See You With

Octopuses may have large eyes for their body size, but a relative of the octopus, the giant squid, has the biggest eye of any animal. It can be 10 inches (25 centimeters) in diameter, the size of a dinner plate.

Camera Eyes

Cameras are basically just artificial eyes that focus images like living eyes do. Light waves are focused on the film instead of a retina. A dial on the camera turns to let in more or less light. This is like the iris

Camera lenses gather and bend light.

of the eye. The lens of the camera is a clear piece of glass or plastic. It gathers and bends light waves and focuses them on the film. Camera lenses are similar to eyeglasses. They are thick, heavy, and curved to focus light, but it is hard to make camera lenses focus exactly right. The sharper the focus, the more curved and heavy an artificial lens must be. Expensive cameras use several different lenses to bend the light, bend it again, and bend it yet again to get the image focused sharply.

Cameras with only one lens, such as cell phone cameras, often take blurry pictures. There is not enough room in a small cell phone camera for several heavy lenses. Besides, such a cell phone camera would be quite expensive.

Baer wondered if he could fix the problems with camera lenses by imitating octopus eyes. He decided to try to copy the structure of octopus lenses to make a better camera.

Fine-Tuning Lenses

The best and most expensive cameras use as many as eight curved lenses to focus sharply under all conditions. A typical 35-millimeter camera needs two or three lenses. A cell phone camera has room for just one small lens.

Expensive digital camera

CHAPTER 3

Inventing Octopus Lenses

Baer and his scientific team wanted to develop a lens made of many layers, like an octopus eye. First they had to find a material that could make good layers. Then they had to put the lens's layers together correctly so that the lens could focus light sharply. In 2004 the scientists succeeded in their invention of an octopus lens. Ever since that time, they have been working to improve the lens so that it can be used in everyday life.

Scientist Eric Baer (pictured) is developing a camera lens that mimics octopus eyes.

Nanotechnology for Lenses

Baer's octopus lens is not a thick, heavy, curved piece of glass. Like the lenses in living eyes, it is made of **nanolayers**. (*Nano* means "one-billionth" and is a measurement used to describe incredibly tiny structures. Nanotechnology is scientific work with making devices almost as small as **molecules**.) In the laboratory, Baer's team used nanotechnology to make layers that were measured in micrometers—millionths

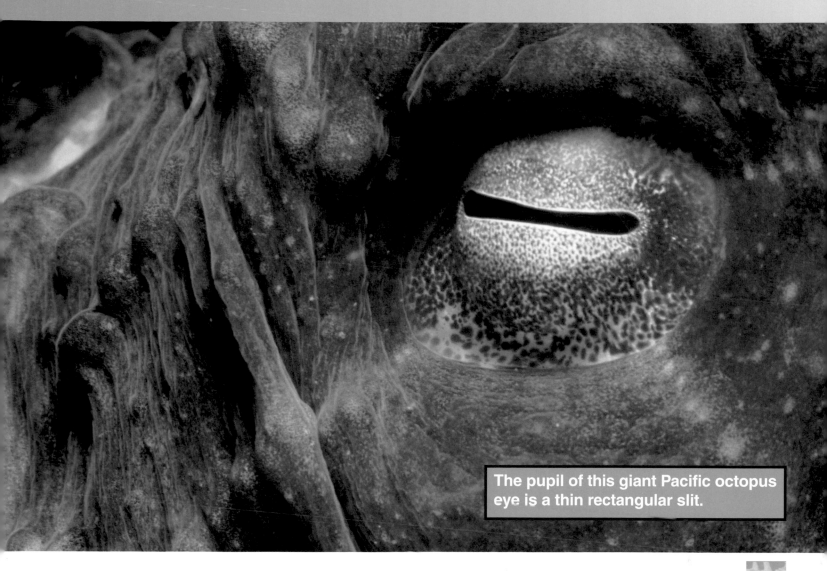

The pupil of this giant Pacific octopus eye is a thin rectangular slit.

The octopus lens compresses thousands of layers of plastic film, similar to the layers of an onion.

of a meter. This work required special instruments and microscopes.

The team used a kind of clear plastic to make extremely thin films to be the layers of their octopus lens. Each film of plastic was only 50 micrometers thick. Baer used these films to build a lens made up of 6,000 nanolayers. Each nanolayer bent light at a slightly different angle. When all the nanolayers were stacked together, like the layers of an onion, the team had made a lens that focused just as an octopus lens does.

Pupil Shapes

People have round pupils, as do most animals. Octopus pupils, on the other hand, are square. On a very bright, sunlit day, the pupil becomes a thin rectangle that lets in just enough light.

Octopus Glasses

Baer made himself a pair of eyeglasses with his octopus eye lenses. The glasses work just as well as his normal glasses to correct his vision, even though they are not curved like his real eyeglasses. They are perfectly flat. This means they are lighter than ordinary lenses, because the more curved lenses are, the thicker and heavier they are.

Lenses for eyeglasses are easier to make than lenses for cameras, because camera lenses have to be much stronger. Baer and his team built a lens with nanolayers that is shaped like a ball. It is just as powerful as an octopus lens. It focuses light sharply, even though it weighs four times less than a curved lens. Next the team wants to make the lens smaller and fit it into a real camera. Then they will have a camera that is lightweight and small but takes pictures as well as a large, expensive camera.

In the future, the team wants to add more layers to the lenses for even sharper focusing power. The team also hopes to make the nanolayers out of a soft, flexible plastic that could change focus for different distances by zooming in or out with just a little squeeze.

Who Needs Better Lenses?

Once the lens is perfected, people will have cell phone cameras that can focus on any object and take perfectly clear pictures. The cell phone cameras would cost no more than cell phone cameras of today. Doctors would find octopus lenses valuable,

Hard to Imagine

Eric Baer's nanolayers are so thin that 10,000 of the layers would have to be stacked on top of each other to equal the thickness of a human hair.

too. They could put tiny lightweight movie cameras on the tips of their surgical instruments. With these probes, doctors could search out problems in human bodies without major surgery. The sharp pictures from the cameras would help them diagnose and treat injuries and diseases.

The U.S. military can think of many ways to use octopus lenses. Small cameras could be attached to unmanned missiles and probes, for example. These flying instruments could be directed over enemy territories to spy on troop movements or identify enemy targets.

Cell phone cameras might one day have octopus lenses that take crystal-clear pictures.

Unmanned aircraft like this Predator might one day benefit from cameras with octopus lenses.

PREDATOR B

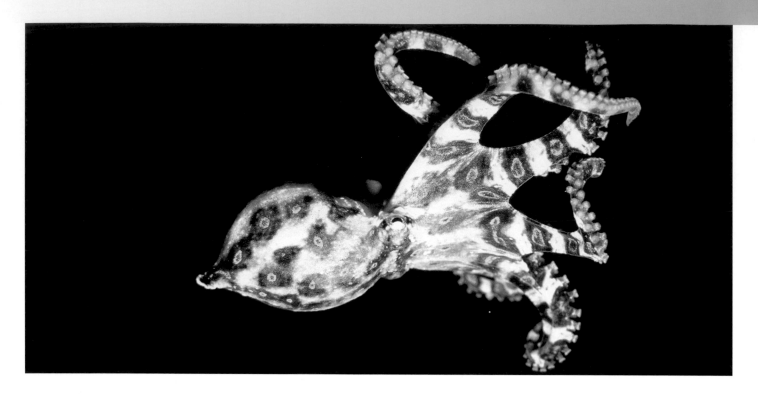

Inspired by the octopus, scientists have created an exciting new camera lens technology.

Seeing with Octopus Power

Baer and his team hope their lenses will be perfected by about 2008. Once the technology is adopted by businesses, the lenses could be included in many kinds of cameras. When that day comes, people will be equipped with powerful tiny cameras that see everything easily, thanks to amazing octopus eyes.

Glossary

cephalopods: Soft-bodied ocean animals that have a large head, large eyes, and tentacles or arms. The octopus, nautilus, and squid are all cephalopods.

contracts: Reduces in size or shrinks.

expands: Increases in size or enlarges.

focus: To cause rays of light waves to come together at a point so that an image is clear and sharp.

iris: The colored part of the eye that controls how much light enters through the pupil.

lens: The clear, curved part of the eye that focuses light. An artificial lens is a clear piece of glass or plastic, usually curved, that also focuses light.

molecules: The tiny basic building blocks of all matter.

nanolayers: Extremely thin films or coatings so small and fine that they are invisible to the human eye.

pupil: The opening in the center of the iris through which light waves pass to the retina.

retina: The membrane inside the eye where images are focused. From the retina, visual information is sent by the optic nerve to the brain.

For Further Exploration

Books

Rebecca L. Johnson, *Nanotechnology*. Minneapolis: Lerner, 2006. Read this book to learn about atoms and molecules and the ways scientists and engineers are manipulating them to invent things for the "nanofuture."

Mary Jo Rhodes, *Octopuses and Squids*. New York: Scholastic Children's Press, 2005. This book discusses the lives of cephalopods—how smart they are, how they use tricks to escape their enemies, and how they raise their babies. Discover some unusual kinds, too, such as the giant octopus and the deep-sea giant squid.

Seymour Simon, *Eyes and Ears*. New York: HarperCollins, 2003. With amazing pictures and clear text, this book explains fascinating facts about how eyes see and how ears hear.

Web Sites

Giant Pacific Octopus, National Parks Conservation Association (www.npca.org/marine_and_coastal/marine_

wildlife/octopus.html). Scientists have discovered that octopuses are intelligent creatures. Visit this site to learn some fun facts about what these octopuses living in the Pacific Ocean can do.

Interview with an Octopus, The Master of Disguise, Tree of Life Web Project (http://tolweb. org/treehouses/?treehouse_id=3382). This site has some fascinating facts about octopuses as told from this imaginary expert—an octopus answering interview questions from Suzie Fish.

Optics for Kids: Science and Engineering, by Bruce Irving, Optical Research Associates (www.opticalres.com/kidoptx.html). Optics is the science of light. At this large site, students can learn about light waves, eyes, lenses, artificial lenses, magnifying glasses, and lasers. Lots of pictures and diagrams make this a very interesting site.

Pringles Pinhole, Science Explorer (www.explora torium.edu/science_explorer/pringles_pinhole.h tml). Learn how to make a real camera that focuses light waves. It is built with simple tools and a potato chip can. Learn why it works, too.

Video Gallery: Octopus Vulgaris, CephBase (www.cephbase.utmb.edu/viddb/vidsrch3.cfm?ID=132). Watch a short video of a camouflaged octopus reacting to the camera.

Vision Abnormalities, ThinkQuest (http://library.thinkquest.org/J002330/visabnor.htm). With many clear drawings, this site explains how focusing problems cause blurry vision and how eyeglasses can correct the problems.

From Octopus Eyes to Powerful Lenses

Index

Picture Credits

Cover: (From left to right) © Stuart Westmorland/Corbis; © Marisa Breyer; © Jeffery L. Rotman/Corbis

© AFP/Getty Images, 6
Courtesy of Case Western Reserve University, 18
© Gary Bell/Corbis, 24
© George Grall/National Geographic/Getty Images, 15
© Getty Images, 23
© Jeff Rotman/Photo Researchers, Inc., 9 (top left)
© Jeffery L. Rotman/Corbis, 8, 19
© Marisa Breyer, 4, 12, 14, 16, 17, 22
Patrick Giles, 13
Photos.com, 20
© Stuart Westmorland/Corbis, 5, 7, 9 (bottom right), 10

About the Author

Toney Allman holds degrees from Ohio State University and the University of Hawaii. She currently lives in Virginia, where she enjoys learning about the natural world and writing books for students.